Math Matters!

Mental Arithmetic

Look out for these sections to help you learn more about each topic:

Remember…
This provides a summary of the key concept(s) on each two-page entry. Use it to revise what you have learned.

Word check
These are new and important words that help you understand the ideas presented on each two-page entry.

All of the word check entries in this book are shown in the glossary on page 45. The versions in the glossary are sometimes more extensive explanations.

Book link…
Although this book can be used on its own, other titles in the *Math Matters!* set may provide more information on certain topics. This section tells you which other titles to refer to.

Place value

To make it easy for you to see exactly what we are doing, you will find colored columns behind the numbers in all the examples on this and the following pages. This is what the colors mean:

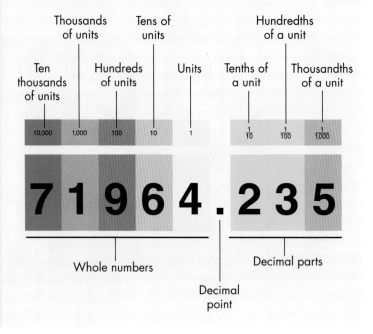

Ten thousands of units — 10,000
Thousands of units — 1,000
Hundreds of units — 100
Tens of units — 10
Units — 1
Tenths of a unit — $\frac{1}{10}$
Hundredths of a unit — $\frac{1}{100}$
Thousandths of a unit — $\frac{1}{1,000}$

7 1 9 6 4 . 2 3 5

Whole numbers

Decimal parts

Decimal point

Series concept by *Brian Knapp and Duncan McCrae*
Text contributed by *Brian Knapp and Colin Bass*
Design and production by *Duncan McCrae*
Illustrations of characters by *Nicolas Debon*
Digital illustrations by *David Woodroffe*
Other illustrations by *Peter Bull Art Studio*
Editing by *Lorna Gilbert and Barbara Carragher*
Layout by *Duncan McCrae and Mark Palmer*
Reprographics by *Global Colour*
Printed and bound by *LEGO SpA, Italy*

First Published in the United States in 1999 by Grolier Educational, Sherman Turnpike, Danbury, CT 06816

Copyright © 1999
Atlantic Europe Publishing Company Limited

Library of Congress Cataloging-in-Publication Data
Math Matters!
    p. cm.
    Includes indexes.
    Contents: v.1.Numbers — v.2.Adding — v.3.Subtracting — v.4.Multiplying — v.5.Dividing — v.6.Decimals — v.7.Fractions – v.8.Shape — v.9.Size — v.10.Tables and Charts — v.11.Grids and Graphs — v.12.Chance and Average — v.13.Mental Arithmetic
ISBN 0–7172–9294–0 (set: alk. paper). — ISBN 0–7172–9295–9 (v.1: alk. paper). — ISBN 0–7172–9296–7 (v.2: alk. paper). — ISBN 0–7172–9297–5 (v.3: alk. paper). — ISBN 0–7172–9298–3 (v.4: alk. paper). — ISBN 0–7172–9299–1 (v.5: alk. paper). — ISBN 0–7172–9300–9 (v.6: alk. paper). — ISBN 0–7172–9301–7 (v.7: alk. paper). — ISBN 0–7172–9302–5 (v.8: alk. paper). — ISBN 0–7172–9303–3 (v.9: alk. paper). — ISBN 0–7172–9304–1 (v.10: alk. paper). — ISBN 0–7172–9305–X (v.11: alk. paper). — ISBN 0–7172–9306–8 (v.12: alk. paper). — ISBN 0–7172–9307–6 (v.13: alk. paper).

    1. Mathematics — Juvenile literature. [1. Mathematics.]
I. Grolier Educational Corporation.
QA40.5.M38   1998
510 — dc21   98–7404
                                                  CIP
                                                  AC

Contents

Introduction

Mental arithmetic means doing simple math in your head. It's what we do every day. Some people, however, are very skilled at it. Take bank managers, for example. They are really used to working accurately with numbers. The older bank managers learned to add in their heads in the days before speedy calculators were in common use. Even today, if you pit one of these people against a calculator, the bank manager will more than likely win. The reason is that the bank manager doesn't have to key in the numbers and so avoids this time-consuming business.

In fact, one bank manager was so fast that he could do a magic card trick in just the same way magicians do today. This is what he would do after dinner as a party treat. He would shuffle a pack of playing cards and spread them out face down so

$42 - 17 = ?$
$= 30 - 5$
$= 25$

$$5 \times 4 \times 3 \times 2 = 20 \times 6 = 120$$

48 + 16 = 50 + 14 = 64

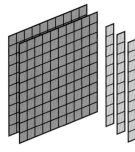

that the value of the cards could not be seen. He would then ask a member of his home audience to pick a card. Then he would turn all the cards over and "riffle" through them. He would do it a second time and then instantly tell the participant what card they held. This was not a trick – it was sheer brain power. How was it done? By adding the numbers on all the cards quickly in his head!

And you too will find that the more you do mental arithmetic, the better and faster you become at it. There's no point in trying to do a problem one way, then thinking it's really hard, and giving up. The trick is to learn some simple skills and use them over and over and over again. It's only when you have practiced that you will suddenly realize that you are much faster than you ever thought possible.

64
+ 73
+ 36
= 173

Score 113

Using pictures

To do arithmetic well in your head, it often helps to find easy ways of calculating. One way is to turn numbers into pictures. Here are some numbers and pictures side by side.

To add **8 + 5**, imagine 8 as a row of 8 counters and 5 as a row of 5 counters below it:

8 ⬤ ⬤ ⬤ ⬤ ⬤ ⬤ ⬤ ⬤

5　　　 ⬤ ⬤ ⬤ ⬤ ⬤

It is quicker to add in your head easy numbers like **10**, so imagine taking 2 from the lower row and adding it to the top row to make a **10**. This leaves **3** on the bottom row.

10 ⬤ ⬤ ⬤ ⬤ ⬤ ⬤ ⬤ ⬤ ⬤ ⬤

3　　　 ⬤ ⬤ ⬤

In this way we have used pictures in our head to work out this sum:

8 + 5 = 10 + 3 = 13

Different people see different shortcuts. Here are some more examples. Look at the numbers and also the pictures, if that helps:

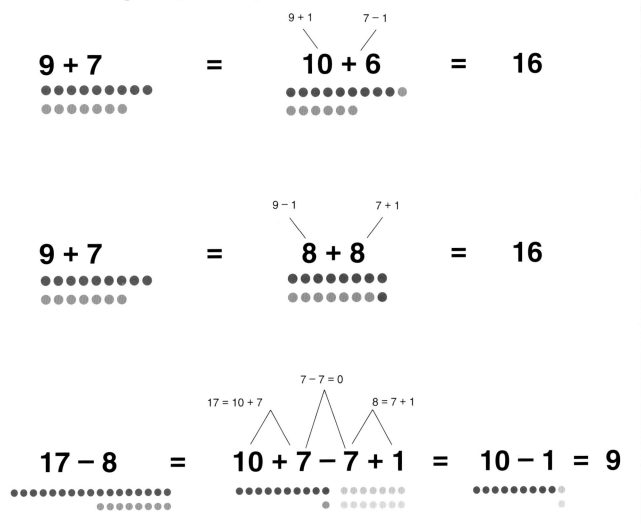

Remember... The idea is to imagine a number as a row of pictures. Move the pictures around in your imagination to get easy numbers like **10** to work with.

Word check

Arithmetic: Simple mathematics with numbers (adding, subtracting, multiplying, and dividing).

Number: One or more numerals placed together represent the size of something (e.g., 45 is the numerals four and five placed together to represent the number forty-five).

Splitting up numbers

The key idea in mental arithmetic is to split up difficult numbers into easy ones.

A large number can be difficult to imagine. But a smaller number is much easier. So, when you see a big number, break it down into smaller ones like this:

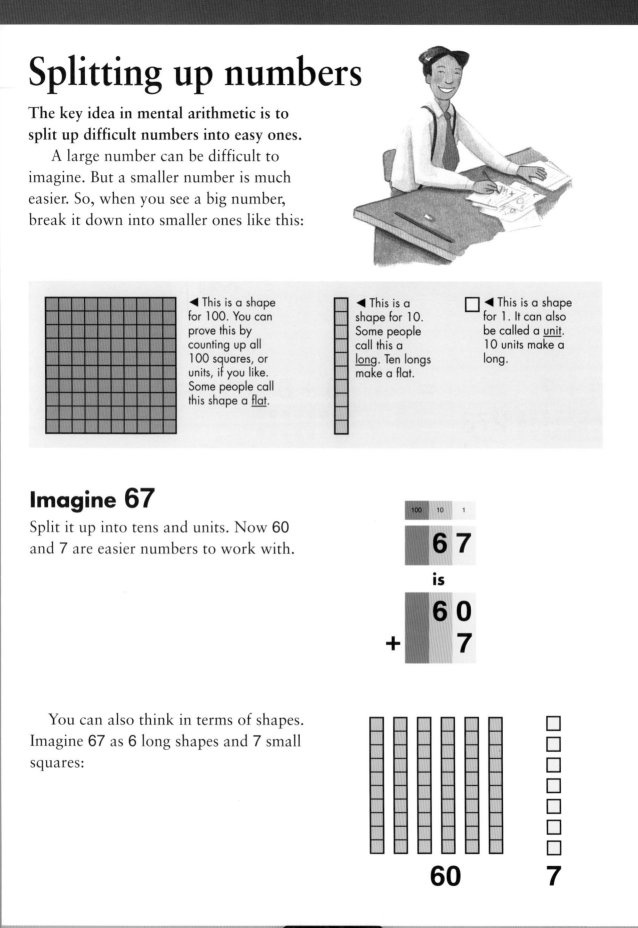

◄ This is a shape for 100. You can prove this by counting up all 100 squares, or units, if you like. Some people call this shape a <u>flat</u>.

◄ This is a shape for 10. Some people call this a <u>long</u>. Ten longs make a flat.

◄ This is a shape for 1. It can also be called a <u>unit</u>. 10 units make a long.

Imagine 67

Split it up into tens and units. Now 60 and 7 are easier numbers to work with.

100	10	1

6 7

is

6 0
+ **7**

You can also think in terms of shapes. Imagine 67 as 6 long shapes and 7 small squares:

60   **7**

Imagine 576

Split up the hundreds, tens, and units.

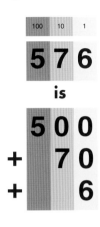

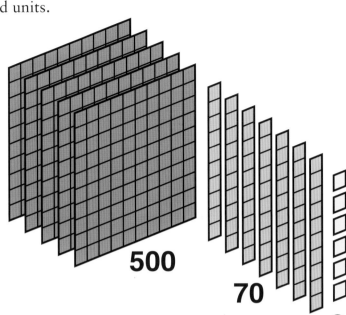

500

70

6

Imagine 273

Split up the hundreds, tens, and units.

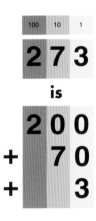

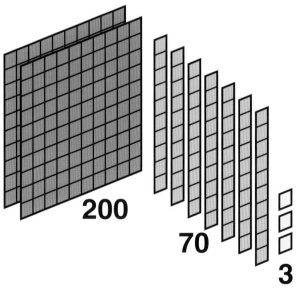

200

70

3

Remember... The key idea in mental arithmetic is to split up difficult numbers into easy ones.

Word check

Mental arithmetic: Simple working with numbers in your head.

Splitting up: Separating numbers into their parts. For example, 67 becomes 60 (just the tens) and 7 (just the units). This makes them easier to work with.

Unit: 1 of something. A small, square shape representing 1.

Put the big numbers first

It is often easier to put the bigger number first wherever this is possible. You can do this because of the Turn-Around Rule.

When you are <u>adding</u> two numbers, it is often easier to add the smaller to the larger. For example, working out:

7 + 23 = ?

is easier if you think of it as:

23 + 7

This is partly because you can more easily think of it as 20 + 3 + 7.

(Answer: 7 + 23 = 23 + 7 = 30)

▼ **If you can think in pictures, this is how you can see the addition.**

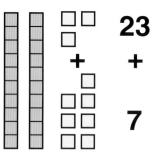

Similarly,

9 + 47 = ?

is easier if you think of it as:

47 + 9

This is because you can then think of it as 47 + 3 + 6. It is then easy to add 47 + 3 = 50 and then 6 more.

(Answer: 9 + 47 = 47 + 9 = 47 + 3 + 6 = 56)

▼ **If you think in numbers, then imagine the colored columns.**

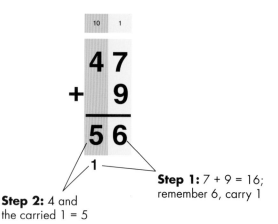

Step 1: 7 + 9 = 16; remember 6, carry 1

Step 2: 4 and the carried 1 = 5

It also helps to put the big numbers first when you <u>multiply</u> numbers. For example, working out:

4 × 25

is easier if you think of it as:

25 × 4

(Answer: 4 × 25 = 25 × 4 = 100)

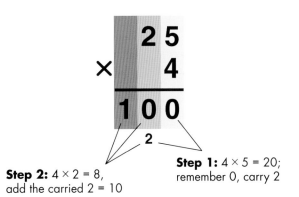

Step 2: 4 × 2 = 8, add the carried 2 = 10

Step 1: 4 × 5 = 20; remember 0, carry 2

Here is another example:

7 × 39

is easier if you think of it as:

39 × 7

(Answer: 7 × 39 = 39 × 7 = 273)

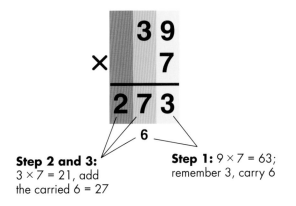

Step 2 and 3: 3 × 7 = 21, add the carried 6 = 27

Step 1: 9 × 7 = 63; remember 3, carry 6

Remember... When adding or multiplying, put the big numbers first to make a calculation easier to work out.

Book link... To find out more about the Turn-Around Rule, see the books *Adding* and *Multiplying* in the *Math Matters!* set.

Work check

Turn-Around Rule: When we add or multiply the same two numbers, the answer is the same no matter which of the numbers comes first (but this does not hold for subtracting or dividing).

Carrying: In adding or multiplying, when the working column total is bigger than 10, this is the method of adding the left digit at the bottom of the column on the left.

Choosing easy pairs

The more numbers there are to deal with, the harder the problem can seem. We need to organize the problem into easy stages.

One way to do this is to look along the row of numbers and see if we can find easy pairs to do first.

Remember, this scheme works only with adding and multiplying.

Look at

37 + 29 + 1

do these numbers first.

29 + 1 = 30

Then you have:

37 + 30 = 67

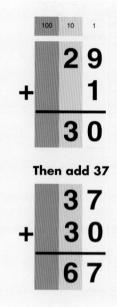

The same is true with

19 + 6 + 12 + 3

do the even numbers first

6 + 12 = 18

Then you have

19 + 18 + 3

Now add the odd numbers:

19 + 3 = 22

Then you have

22 + 18 = 40

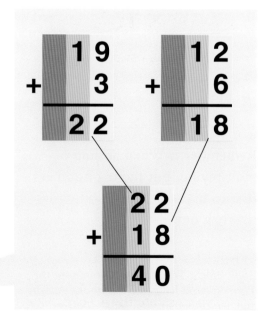

The same principle works with multiplying:

$$14 \times 25 \times 4$$

We could first work out:

$$14 \times 25$$

(which comes to 350)
and then multiply:

$$350 \times 4$$

(which comes to 1,400).
But instead, we can work out the answer in a different, and easier, order.

For example, we know that:

$$25 \times 4 = 100$$

So we can do this part of the working out first.

Then we can work out:

$$14 \times 100 = 1,400$$

which is very easy indeed.

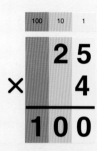

100	10	1
	2	5
×		4
1	**0**	**0**

Then times by 14:

1,000	100	10	1
		1	4
×	1	0	0
1	**4**	**0**	**0**

Notice that this multiplication has the bigger number underneath. This is the only time we do this, because multiplying by 100 is simply a matter of adding two 0's to the first number.

Remember... You can add or multiply in any order to make things as easy as possible for yourself.

Word check
Row: Things placed side by side. In a table the entries that are in any line across the page.

Work with even numbers first

Many problems can be made simpler by working with even numbers first.

For example:

64 + 73 + 36 = ?

This is a mixture of even and odd numbers.

Because it is often easier to work with even numbers first, we group the even numbers together:

64 + 36 + 73 = ?

Now add the two even numbers, 64 and 36:

64 + 36 = 100

But if you found this hard to do in your head, you can think of the numbers split up like this:

60 + 4 + 30 + 6

Adding easy pairs (see page 12),

60 + 30 = 90 and **4 + 6 = 10**

brings us to:

90 + 10 = 100

Finally, add in the odd number, 73:

100 + 73 = 173

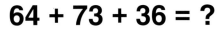

Word check
Even number: A multiple of 2.
Odd number: A number that cannot be divided by 2.

To add 64 and 36, either:

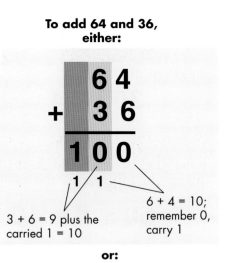

$$\begin{array}{r} 6\ 4 \\ +\quad 3\ 6 \\ \hline 1\ 0\ 0 \end{array}$$

3 + 6 = 9 plus the carried 1 = 10

6 + 4 = 10; remember 0, carry 1

or:

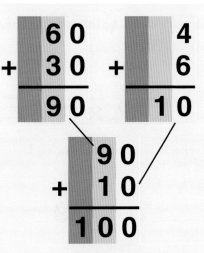

$$\begin{array}{r} 6\ 0 \\ +\quad 3\ 0 \\ \hline 9\ 0 \end{array} \qquad \begin{array}{r} 4 \\ +\quad 6 \\ \hline 1\ 0 \end{array}$$

$$\begin{array}{r} 9\ 0 \\ +\quad 1\ 0 \\ \hline 1\ 0\ 0 \end{array}$$

Then add 73:

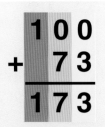

$$\begin{array}{r} 1\ 0\ 0 \\ +\quad 7\ 3 \\ \hline 1\ 7\ 3 \end{array}$$

Here is another example:

16 + 29 + 58 = ?

As in the previous example, we rearrange the order in our heads and begin to work out:

16 + 58 + 29 = ?

It is easier to add smaller numbers to larger ones, so rearrange again:

58 + 16 = 74

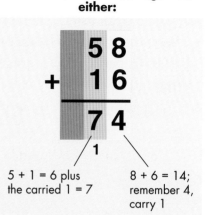

To add 16, 29 and 58 together, either:

$$
\begin{array}{r}
58 \\
+\ 16 \\
\hline
74 \\
\end{array}
$$

1

5 + 1 = 6 plus the carried 1 = 7

8 + 6 = 14; remember 4, carry 1

Again, if you found this hard to do in your head, you can think of the numbers split up like this:

50 + 8 + 10 + 6

Adding easy pairs:

50 + 10 = 60 and **8 + 6 = 14**

brings us to:

60 + 14 = 74

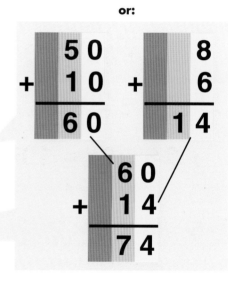

or:

$$
\begin{array}{r}
50 \\
+\ 10 \\
\hline
60 \\
\end{array}
\qquad
\begin{array}{r}
8 \\
+\ 6 \\
\hline
14 \\
\end{array}
$$

$$
\begin{array}{r}
60 \\
+\ 14 \\
\hline
74 \\
\end{array}
$$

Now add in the odd number, 29:

74 + 29

= 70 + 4 + 20 + 9

= 90 + 13 = 103

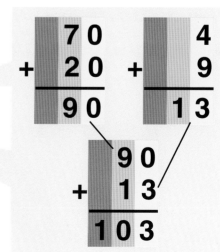

Then add the odd numbers:

$$
\begin{array}{r}
70 \\
+\ 20 \\
\hline
90 \\
\end{array}
\qquad
\begin{array}{r}
4 \\
+\ 9 \\
\hline
13 \\
\end{array}
$$

$$
\begin{array}{r}
90 \\
+\ 13 \\
\hline
103 \\
\end{array}
$$

Remember... Look to see whether any of the numbers in the problem "fit together" easily.

Multiply odd by even numbers

Multiplying can often seem hard because the numbers appear awkward.

For most people it is a great help to multiply odd numbers by even numbers (not even numbers by odd numbers).

Multiplying odd by even helps in simple multiplications like this:

5 × 4 × 3 × 2 = ?

Because

5 × 4 = 20

and

3 × 2 = 6

so

5 × 4 × 3 × 2

= 20 × 6

= 120

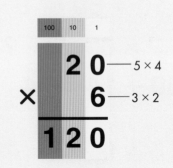

To see why this is easier, let's try multiplying:

8 × 7 × 6 × 5 = ?

First reverse 8 × 7:

8 × 7 = 7 × 8 = 56

Then reverse 6 × 5:

6 × 5 = 5 × 6 = 30

We are left with:

56 × 30

Since this is a one-line multiplication (56 × 3, then add 0 to the answer), it is easy to do in your head.

= 1,680

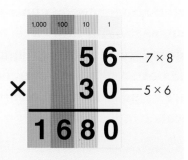

Suppose for the same sum:

8 × 7 × 6 × 5 = ?

we had multiplied odds together and evens together. In this case we first reverse then multiply the even numbers 8 × 6:

8 × 6 = 6 × 8 = 48

Then reverse and multiply the odd numbers 7 × 5:

7 × 5 = 5 × 7 = 35

We now multiply the results:

48 × 35

This is much harder to do in your head, as the multiplication on the right shows.

= 1,680

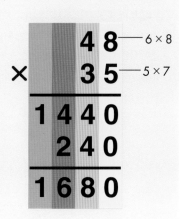

Quick wits at the market

This story example shows how you can use a number of the ideas we have shown you on the previous pages. Notice that Fatima was in a busy market, the sort of place where it is very handy to be able to calculate in your head.

The tea set

Fatima had a very pretty porcelain tea set for six people. Over the years three of the cups and three of the saucers had been broken.

One day, while Fatima was looking around an antiques market in New Orleans, she saw a stall selling matching pieces to her tea set quite cheaply. Cups were priced at $5.60 and saucers at $3.40.

Fatima told the assistant that she wanted three cups and three saucers. While the assistant was busy with her calculator, Fatima checked the answer in her head.

First, she converted the dollars and cents into cents by multiplying by 100. Then she ignored the currency sign:

5.60 = 560; 3.40 = 340

Then, instead of multiplying first, she added first.

She grouped the prices of one cup and one saucer:

$$560 \text{ (a cup)} + 340 \text{ (a saucer)}$$

Then to calculate the sum, she turned the big numbers into easier ones by splitting up the big numbers:

$$= 500 + 300 + 60 + 40$$

Then she added easy pairs:

$$= 800 + 100$$
$$= 900$$

Next, because she wanted three cups and three saucers, she multiplied the price of a single cup and saucer by 3:

$$900 \times 3 = 2{,}700$$

Finally, she divided by 100 and put back the currency sign. Fatima now knew that she owed $27.00.

Book link... Find out more about working with decimals in the book *Decimals* in the *Math Matters!* set.

Remember... To group numbers, add in the easiest order and then multiply. Always work without decimal points or currency signs.

Word check
Currency: The money generally used in a country, such as dollars ($), pounds (£), yen (¥).
Pair: Two things that match up in some way.

When adding is better than multiplying

It can be easier to add in what at first seems to be a multiplication problem.

Here we split our numbers to make the multiplication easier, then add the results.

You can think of the numbers we use to make the calculation easier as "stepping stones," making a difficult large single step easier by separating it into a number of smaller steps.

Multiply:

$$26 \times 4 = ?$$

First:

split 26 into 25 + 1

because 25's are easy to work with. Now we can multiply each part by 4 like this:

$$25 \times 4 = 100$$
$$1 \times 4 = 4$$

and add the results:

$$100 + 4 = 104$$

What is:

$$125 \times 5 = ?$$

We are going to split the 5 up into 4 + 1 and then split the 125 up into 100 + 25 so that we can use the 4 and the 100 as stepping stones to making our calculation easier.

Follow these steps:

Step 1: Split the numbers up into:

$$= (125 \times 4) + (125 \times 1)$$
$$= (125 \times 4) + 125$$

Step 2: Now split the 125 into 100 and 25:

$$= (100 \times 4 + 25 \times 4) + 125$$

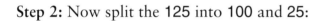

125

Step 3: Now work out what is in the brackets:

100×4 25×4

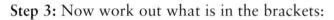

$$= (400 + 100) + 125$$

$$= 500 + 125$$

$$= 625$$

Remember... If the numbers in a problem appear difficult, you might be able to split up one or more of them so that they will be easier to work with.

Word check

Stepping stones: Easy numbers used to simplify finding your way through a calculation you are doing in your head.

Many ways to add

If you split a number up when adding, it often makes a sum easier to work out. There are several ways you can do it. Here are four ways to work out:

48 + 16 = ?

See which one you find easiest.

Example 1

Think of the **16** as **2 + 14**

So the starting calculation can be shown as:

48 + 2 + 14

Now add easy pairs, 48 and 2, making the calculation:

50 + 14

Now you have two more simple numbers to add together:

50 + 14 = 64

Example 2

Think of the **16** as **20 − 4**

So the starting calculation can be shown as:

48 + 20 − 4

Now add 20 to 48, making the calculation:

68 − 4

Now you have an easy subtraction:

68 − 4 = 64

Example 3

Think of the **48** as **50 − 2**

So the starting calculation can be shown as:

50 + 16 − 2

Now add 16 to 50, making the calculation:

66 − 2

This leaves an easy subtraction:

66 − 2 = 64

Example 4

Think of the numbers as shapes. Imagine adding 2 of the 16 to the 48, making 50 and leaving 14.

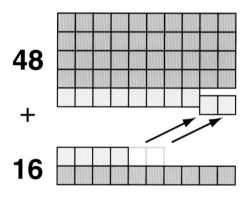

48

+

16

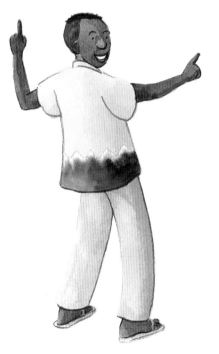

Remember... Start by finding an easy way to think about the numbers you are working with.

Word check
Easy pair: Pairs of numbers that make easy answers, such as 2 + 8 = 10, 48 + 2 = 50

Several ways to subtract

There are several different ways of subtracting in your head. Here the starting numbers have been split differently in each method.

Three ways can be used to work out:

$$42 - 17 = ?$$

Example 1

Separate **17** into **12** and **5**

So the starting calculation can be shown as:

$$= 42 - 12 - 5$$

Now subtract 12 from 42, which is simple because the last digits are both 2:

$$42 - 12 = 30$$

Finally subtract 5 from the 30:

$$= 30 - 5$$
$$= 25$$

Example 2

Separate $\boxed{17}$ into **2** and **15**

So the starting calculation can be shown as:
42 – 2 – 15

Now subtract 2 from 42 which is simple because the last digits are the same:
42 – 2 = 40

This makes the calculation:
= 40 – 15
= 25

Example 3

Separate $\boxed{42}$ into **22** and **20**

So the starting calculation can be shown as:
20 + 22 – 17

Now subtract 17 from 22, which is 5:
= 22 – 17 = 5

This makes the calculation:
= 20 + 5
= 25

Remember... See if you can separate the starting numbers into numbers that are easier to work with.

Word check

Digit: The numerals 1, 2, 3, 4, 5, 6, 7, 8, 9, or 0. Several may be used to stand for a larger number. They are called digits to make it clear that they are only part of a complete number. So we might say, "The second digit is 4," meaning the second numeral from the left. Or we might say, "That is a two-digit number," meaning that it has two numerals in it, tens and units.

Subtracting by adding on

You can find the difference between two numbers by adding on from the smaller one.

We often add on to help check that we are right. For example, if you are given 100 sweets for a party and only need 73, you might say: 73 and 2 is 75, and 5 is 80, and 10 is 90, and 10 more is 100. As 2 and 5 and 10 and 10 make 27, so you know that the difference between 100 and 73 is 27.

You can use this adding method to help you do any kind of mental subtraction, for example, to subtract 73 cm from 100 cm.

Note: It works best if you are taking away <u>from</u> an easy number, like 100, or even a much bigger easy number.

Example 1

Katie and Lucy were playing a word game. Katie had 92 points, and Lucy had only 37. How many did Lucy have to score to catch up?

Here we are adding on from the smaller number again. Start at 30. Find a number, such as 3, that adds to 37 to make an easy number to remember.

37 and 3 is 40

Remember 3 as the first part of our final answer. The next jump can be to add an easy number 50, which brings us close to 92.

40 and 50 is 90

Remember 50 + 3 = 53 as the second part of our final answer. Now we only have 2 to go:

90 and 2 is 92

Remember 53 + 2 = 55 as the final part of our answer.

So the final answer is: **55 points**

Example 2

Mr. Filton was waiting for a train home. His watch showed 4:23 pm and his train was due to leave at 5:04 pm. How long did he have to wait?

Start by adding a small number to get an answer which is an easy number.

23 + 2 = 25   (4:25pm)

Remember 2 as the first part of our final answer.

Now add 5 to bring us to the half hour:

25 + 5 = 30   (4:30pm)

Remember 2 + 5 = 7 as the second part of our final answer.

Now add on another 30 to bring us to the full hour:

30 + 30 = 60   (5:00pm)

Remember 7 + 30 = 37 as the third part of our final answer.

Now we simply have a final 4 to add to bring us to the time the train will leave:

60 + 4 = 64   (5:04pm)

Remember 37 + 4 = 41 as the final part of our answer. So the time he has to wait is:

41 minutes

Remember... It is often easier to "see" the answer to a subtraction by adding upward from the smaller number. This can also be a good check for subtractions you have written down.

Note: When working out problems which use time we always have to remember that each hour is **60** minutes.

Subtracting across 100

Here is an easy way to subtract from numbers larger than **100**.

Again, it is a matter of making the numbers easy to work out in your head. To see the difference, compare the way used for doing the calculation in your head to the way it would be done on paper.

What is

133 − 85 = ?

To make the numbers easier to work with, split 133 into 100 and 33:

100 + 33 − 85

Now, rearrange the calculation so that we can take 85 from 100:

= 100 − 85 + 33

Next, do the subtraction:

(100 − 85) + 33

(perhaps you might say 85 plus 5 = 90, plus 10 = 100, answer 15 – this is the "adding on" method shown on page 26).

= 15 + 33

This leaves the addition:

15 + 33 = 48

(try 10 + 5 + 30 + 3 to do this. 10 + 30 = 40 and 5 + 3 = 8, so the answer is 48).

▼ **This is how you would write the problem on paper using the exchanging method of subtracting.**

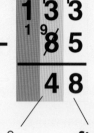

| 100 | 10 | 1 |

$$1\overset{1}{\cancel{3}}\overset{1}{3}$$
$$-\ \overset{19}{\cancel{8}}5$$
$$4\ 8$$

Step 2: 3 − 9 won't work, borrow 1 from the hundreds column. 13 − 9 = 4

Step 1: 3 − 5 won't go, borrow 1 from the tens column. 13 − 5 = 8

Here is another example so that you can see the common steps.

Remember, get the subtraction out of the way by subtracting from an easy number like 100. Then you are left with an addition, which is easy to do in your head:

$$159 - 77 = ?$$

To make the numbers easier to work with, split 159 into 100 and 59:

$$100 + 59 - 77$$

Now, rearrange the calculation so that we can take 77 from 100:

$$= 100 - 77 + 59$$

Next, do the subtraction:

$$(100 - 77) + 59$$

(perhaps you might say 77 plus 3 = 80, plus 20 = 100, answer 23 – this is the "adding on" method shown on page 26).

$$= 23 + 59$$

This leaves the addition:

$$23 + 59 = 82$$

(try 20 + 3 + 50 + 9 to do this 20 + 50 = 70 and 3 + 9 = 12, so the answer is 82).

Remember... The key to subtracting across 100 is to split the number being subtracted from into 100 + the extra above 100.

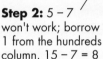

▼ **This is how you would write the problem on paper using the regrouping method of subtracting.**

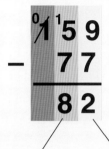

Step 2: 5 – 7 won't work; borrow 1 from the hundreds column. 15 – 7 = 8

Step 1: 9 – 7 = 2

Word check

Rearrange: Moving numbers and their signs around in an equation to make them easier to work with but without altering their value (for example, 3 – 7 + 6 is more easily solved by rearranging to 3 + 6 – 7).

Book link... For more on the exchanging and regrouping methods of subtracting see the book *Subtracting* in the *Math Matters!* set.

Ziggie and Mtoto in Ghana

Ziggie and Mtoto were on vacation in Ghana. On the last afternoon the whole family was looking around the souvenir stores for presents to take back to their friends and relatives. Dad had given each of the twins a **5,000** cedi note to spend.

Both Ziggie and Mtoto found many hand-crafted items they wanted to take home to show their friends. In the end Ziggie found her items cost 3,755 cedi, and Mtoto found his items cost 2,895 cedi.

Before they bought them, Ziggie and Mtoto wanted to work out how much change they would get. Here is a way of solving the problem:

Step 1: To find Ziggie's change from 5,000 cedi we are going to add upwards from 3,755:

3,755 + 5 = 3,760

Remember 5.

3,760 + 40 = 3,800

Now we have added 5 + 40 = 45, so remember 45.

3,800 + 200 = 4,000

Now we have added 200 + 45 = 245, so remember 245.

4,000 + 1,000 = 5,000

In adding upwards to 5,000 we have added 1,000 and 245, so our answer is 1,245 cedi.

1,000 + 245 = 1,245

Step 2: We will also find Mtoto's change from 5,000 cedi by adding upward from 2,895:

$$2,895 + 5 = 2,900$$

Remember 5.

$$2,900 + 100 = 3,000$$

Now we have added 100 + 5 = 105, so remember 105.

$$3,000 + 2,000 = 5,000$$

In adding upwards to 5,000 we have added 2,000 and 105, so our answer is 2,105 cedi.

$$2,000 + 105 = 2,105$$

Step 3: To find Ziggie and Mtoto's change, we have to work out:

$$1,245 + 2,105 = ?$$

First, we want to make the numbers easier to work with before we add them in our head.

Add 5 to the first number, and subtract 5 from the second:

$$1,245 + 5 + 2,105 - 5 = ?$$

This gives:

$$1,250 + 2,100 = 3,350$$

So their change was 3,350 cedi.

Can't remember your tables?

Multiplication tables are single columns of multiplication facts. Put side by side they make a multiplication square.

Most of us forget some parts of our multiplication tables, but here are suggestions of ways to cover up some of the gaps.

Example 1

$$7 \times 8 = ?$$

Step 1: Start by multiplying using 2's:

$$7 \times 2 = 14$$

Step 2: Multiply by 2 again; this is 7×4:

$$14 \times 2 = 28$$

Step 3: Multiply by 2 again; this is 7×8:

$$28 \times 2 = 56$$

So, by multiplying by 2 three times, you get the same answer as multiplying by 8.

Example 2

$$7 \times 9 = ?$$

Step 1: Multiply by 3:

$$7 \times 3 = 21$$

Step 2: Multiply by 3 again:

$$21 \times 3 = 63$$

(this is $7 \times 3 \times 3$, or 7×9).

Therefore, by multiplying by 3 twice, you get the same answer as multiplying by 9.

Here is another way that you can try.
If you know that, for example:

7 × 8 = 56

then

7 × 9

is

56 + 7 = 63

Below is a multiplication square to remind you of any gaps you have in numbers up to 9 × 9. You can copy out and extend this square to 12 × 12 to cover your 12 times tables.

×	1	2	3	4	5	6	7	8	9
1	1	2	3	4	5	6	7	8	9
2	2	4	6	8	10	12	14	16	18
3	3	6	9	12	15	18	21	24	27
4	4	8	12	16	20	24	28	32	36
5	5	10	15	20	25	30	35	40	45
6	6	12	18	24	30	36	42	48	54
7	7	14	21	28	35	42	49	56	63
8	8	16	24	32	40	48	56	64	72
9	9	18	27	36	45	54	63	72	81

Tip... If you cannot remember one multiplication, say 7 × 5, then think of it the other way around, as 5 × 7. This is the Turn-Around Rule (see page 10).

Remember... The square above can be used to find out basic multiplication facts. Suppose you want to find 3 × 5, find 3 from the column marked 3 and 5 from the row marked 5. Now go along the row and column to find where they meet. You will find the answer is 15.

Word check
Multiplication facts: The numbers produced by multiplying together numbers we use a lot, such as 3 × 4 = 12. They are facts we remember rather than work out each time. Some people also refer to these multiplication facts as multiplication tables.

Multiplication square: The multiplication tables arranged into a square shape.

Multiplication tables: Multiplication facts set out in columns.

Column: Things placed one below the other. In a table the entries that are in a line that goes up and down the page.

Using doubles and triples

Many sports and games need rapid, accurate use of mathematics. In international darts, for instance, you need to be quick at multiplying.

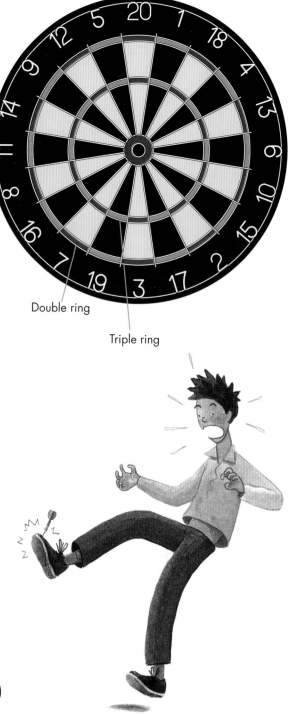

In a singles dart game there are two players, each of whom has three darts, like the ones shown here. The target is a dartboard that is hung on a wall. It is marked off in numbered sectors, as you can see.

The players take turns standing a fixed distance from the board and throwing their darts into it.

Usually, each player starts with a score of 501. The score for each three darts is added up and then subtracted from the remaining score. The first player to reach zero wins.

However, there are some special areas on the board where you can get a bigger score. These are the triple (three times) and double (two times) rings.

The winner must finish by throwing a dart into a double (that means if the player lands in double 19, the score is 38).

Double ring

Triple ring

It was Wayne's turn in the darts game. He had to score 113. First he had to score an odd number, so that the remainder would be an even number, and he could finish on a double. If he scored triple 11 with his first dart, he planned to finish on two double 20's. First triple 11.

$$11 \times 3 = 33$$
$$113 - 33 = 80$$

And then the 2 double 20's.

$$(20 \times 2) + (20 \times 2) = 80$$

Unluckily, he just missed triple 11. Instead the dart went into triple 14. Now he had to do some more quick mental arithmetic: His score was now:

$$3 \times 14 = 42 \qquad {\scriptstyle 3 \times (10 + 4) = 30 + 12}$$

$$113 - 42 = 71 \qquad {\scriptstyle 110 - 40 + 3 - 2 = 70 + 1}$$

If he hit triple 11 this time, his score would become:

$$71 - 33 = 38 \qquad {\scriptstyle 60 + 11 - 30 - 3}$$

Now, 38 is double 19.
Again he missed and instead hit triple 19, which is an odd number.
Triple 19 is:

$$3 \times 19 = 57 \qquad {\scriptstyle 3 \times (20 - 1) = 60 - 3}$$

Wayne used "counting back" to find out what he had to score now:

$$\overset{14}{57 + (3 + 10 + 1)} = 71$$

so he had to score:

14

Score 113

Now, double 7 would do, and to his delight, this is exactly what he got!

Remember… For speedy answers, split up big numbers into simpler ones.

Word check
Score: The word for the total in sports and games.

Halving and adding

Numbers can seem really awkward, but they can be made easier by using fractions and adding.

Some tourists were visiting a shop in Edinburgh, Scotland, when they saw a tartan they really wanted. They discovered it cost £40 before tax. So how much is the tax if the rate is 17.5%?

Now, 17.5% may seem a very awkward number to work with, but it can be made easy like this:

$$17.5 = 10 + 5 + 2.5$$

Since 2.5 is half of 5, and 5 is half of 10, all you really need to be able to do is to divide by 10 and 2:

10% of 40 is a tenth of 40:

$$\frac{40}{10} = 4$$

5% is half of 10%:

$$\frac{4}{2} = 2$$

2.5% is half of 5%:

$$\frac{2}{2} = 1$$

Now we can add these together to give the sales tax:

$$4 + 2 + 1 = 7$$

The price before tax (£40) plus the sales tax (£7) give a total price of £47:

$$40 + 7 = 47$$

Halving and doubling

There is another way that awkward numbers can be made easier. It is called halving and doubling. The tourists could easily have worked out the cost of the tartan they wanted to buy this way, too. Compare this method with the method on the page opposite.

When you are multiplying two numbers, if you halve one and double the other, the answer stays the same.

For the sales tax on the tartan:

$$40 \times 17.5\%$$

40 is an easy number to halve. The answer is 20.
17.5 is an easy number to double. The answer is 35.

$$= 20 \times 35\%$$

Halve 20 and double 35:

$$= 10 \times 70\%$$

Now the multiplication is easier:

$$= 10 \times \frac{70}{100}$$

$$= 7$$

The sales tax is therefore £7.
The total cost of the tartan is the ticket price (£40) and the sales tax (£7). This is £47:

$$40 + 7 = 47$$

Remember... Halving a number is often the key to making the number easier to work with.

Word check

%: The symbol for percent.

Percent: A number followed by the % symbol means the number is divided by 100. It is a way of writing a fraction.

Sales tax: A percentage added on to the cost of things that are bought. The extra money is then used by the government.

Near doubles

Doubling can often save time. Here is how to use doubling when the numbers to multiply are just **1** apart.

Two tourists, Susie and Tom, went to Orlando, Florida, and found they needed new sunglasses. They saw a matching pair they liked. The ladies' style cost $16, but the men's version cost $17. The two prices were just 1 apart.

Susie worked out the total by doubling the first number and adding 1.

$$16 \times 2 + 1$$
$$= 32 + 1$$
$$= 33$$

This is the "near-double" principle.

Or, Susie could have worked out:

$$17 \times 2 - 1$$
$$= 34 - 1$$
$$= 33$$

That is, she could have doubled the second number and then subtracted 1.

$$
\begin{array}{r}
1\ 6 \\
+\ 1\ 7 \\
\hline
3\ 3 \\
\end{array}
$$
1

Near doubles, halving, and adding

Susie and Tom were expecting to pay $33 for their sunglasses, but they knew that sales tax had to be added on. It was 6%. Tom checked the amount of the tax like this:

$$6\% = (5 + 1)\%$$

Now, 5% is half of 10%, and 10% of 33 is a tenth of 33.00, or 3.30:

This meant that Tom could calculate that if 10% of 33.00 is 3.30, then 5% is <u>half</u> of 3.30:

$$\frac{3.30}{2} = 1.65$$

And because 1% is a tenth of 10% then he worked out that 1% of 33 was:

$$\frac{3.30}{10} = 0.33$$

By adding these two answers together Tom worked out that 6% tax on $33 is $1.98:

$$1.65 + 0.33 = 1.98$$

The total cost of the sunglasses was therefore the price ($33) plus the sales tax ($1.98).
This was $34.98.

Remember... Splitting up numbers to make doubles can save time and make numbers easier to work with.

More near equals

If you can remember square numbers, here you have another way to remember awkward multiplication facts.

Imagine that we have a square like a chess board.

It is **8 × 8 = 64**

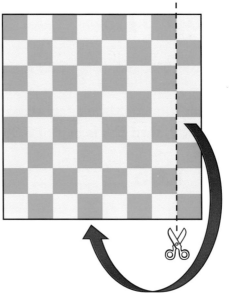

Then we cut one row of squares off the edge. Next, we stick that row along another edge. Our square then becomes a rectangle of **9** units (or squares) by **7**, with an odd bit sticking out at the corner.

We cut this odd bit off and throw it away.

The area of the rectangle we have made is **9 × 7**. This is **64 − 1**, because we took one square away.

So **9 × 7 = 63**

You could do this starting with a square of any size. For example:

$$6 \times 6 - 1 = 7 \times 5$$
$$4 \times 4 - 1 = 5 \times 3$$

You can see that by cutting the edge off a square as we did on page 40, that this trick works however big the numbers are. So now we know that:

$$19 \times 21 = 20 \times 20 - 1$$
$$= 400 - 1 = 399$$

and:

$$16 \times 14 = 15 \times 15 - 1$$
$$= 225 - 1 = 224$$

and:

$$99 \times 101 = 100 \times 100 - 1$$
$$= 10,000 - 1 = 9,999$$

When you come across a large square number, it is worth trying to remember it for use in this trick.

Remember... This trick is useful when the "near equal" numbers are 2 units apart, and you know the square of the number between them.

Word check

Square number: The number of a collection of objects that can be arranged in a square. It is the product of two equal numbers (for example, 16 is the square number produced from 4×4).

Rectangle: A four-sided shape in which pairs of opposite sides are the same length and all four corners are right angles.

The Wordsmith's card game

Here is an example where you can use many of the mental arithmetic rules you have seen on the previous pages. They are set out below as part of a family card game.

The Wordsmith family is playing a card game. Each player has seven letter cards and takes turns to make up a sort of a crossword.

It is Ziggie's turn, and she thinks she can make an eight-letter word using an L already on the board and adding an A to WASH to make it AWASH. If she can do this, she can score 173 points.

At present, Ziggie's father is in the lead with 335 points, and Ziggie is second with 166.

Will Ziggie overtake her father?

To find out, we need to know if:

335 − 166 > 173

First find some "stepping stones" to make the subtraction easier. In this case we will use 300 (because it is close to 335) and 200 (because it is close to 166) as "stepping stones" to the answer. Remember, we have to add and subtract the 300 and the 200 to leave the equation unchanged.

$$= 335 + (-300 + 300) + (-200 + 200) - 166$$

Now we can take away more easily:

$$= (335 - 300) + (300 - 200) + (200 - 166)$$

(335 − 300 = 35; 300 − 200 = 100). To find 200 − 166, we count up: 4 to 170 and 30 more to 200.

$$= 35 + 100 + (4 + 30)$$

Now use the Turn-Around Rule to add numbers in the easiest order:

$$= 100 + 35 + 34$$

And finally, because 35 and 34 are close, use the technique of near doubles ($35 + 34 = 35 \times 2 - 1$):

$$= 100 + 35 \times 2 - 1$$
$$= 169$$

Since 173 is bigger than 169, a score of 173 would just put Ziggie into the lead. So she decides to risk it and puts down the cards to spell ATLANTIC.

Word check

> : The symbol for more than.

Near doubles: The sum of two numbers that are just 1 apart is twice (double) the larger number minus one.

What symbols mean

Here is a list of the common math symbols together with an example of how they are used. You will find this list in each of the *Math Matters!* books, so that you can turn to any book if you want to look up the meaning of a symbol.

— Between two numbers this symbol means "subtract" or "minus." In front of one number it means the number is negative. In Latin *minus* means "less."

+ The symbol for adding. We say it "plus." In Latin *plus* means "more."

✕ The symbol for multiplying. We say it "multiplied by" or "times."

= The symbol for equals. We say it "equals" or "makes." It comes from a Latin word meaning "level" because weighing scales are level when the amounts on each side are equal.

$$(8 + 9 - 3) \times \frac{2}{5} = 5.6$$

( ) Parentheses. You do everything inside the parentheses first. Parentheses always occur in pairs.

—, /, and **÷** Three symbols for dividing. We say it "divided by." A pair of numbers above and below a / or — make a fraction, so ⅖ or $\frac{2}{5}$ is the fraction two-fifths.

■ This is a decimal point. It is a dot written after the units when a number contains parts of a unit as well as whole numbers. This is the decimal number five point six or five and six-tenths.

Glossary

Other symbols in this book.

%: The symbol for percent.

> : The symbol for more than.

Terms commonly used in this book.

Adding on: Finding the difference between two numbers by adding on from the smaller one.

Arithmetic: Simple mathematics with numbers (adding, subtracting, multiplying, and dividing).

Carrying: In adding or multiplying, when the working column total is bigger than 10, this is the method of adding the left digit at the bottom of the column on the left.

Column: Things placed one below the other. In a table the entries that are in a line that goes up and down the page.

Currency: The money generally used in a country, such as dollars ($), pounds (£), yen (¥).

Digit: The numerals 1, 2, 3, 4, 5, 6, 7, 8, 9, or 0. Several may be used to stand for a larger number. They are called digits to make it clear that they are only part of a complete number. So we might say, "The second digit is 4," meaning the second numeral from the left. Or we might say, "That is a two-digit number," meaning that it has two numerals in it, tens and units.

Easy pair: Pairs of numbers that make easy answers, such as 2 + 8 = 10, 48 + 2 = 50.

Even number: A multiple of 2.

Mental arithmetic: Simple working with numbers in your head.

Multiplication facts: The numbers produced by multiplying together numbers we use a lot, such as 3 × 4 = 12. They are facts we remember rather than work out each time. Some people also refer to these multiplication facts as multiplication tables.

Multiplication square: The multiplication tables arranged into a square shape.

Multiplication tables: Multiplication facts set out in columns.

Near doubles: The sum of two numbers that are just 1 apart is twice (double) the larger number minus one.

Number: One or more numerals placed together represent the size of something (e.g., 45 is the numerals four and five placed together to represent the number forty-five).

Odd number: A number that cannot be divided by 2.

Pair: Two things that match up in some way.

Percent: A number followed by the % symbol means the number is divided by 100. It is a way of writing a fraction.

Rearrange: Moving numbers and their signs around in an equation to make them easier to work with but without altering their value (for example, 3 − 7 + 6 is more easily solved by rearranging to 3 + 6 − 7).

Rectangle: A four-sided shape in which pairs of opposite sides are the same length and all four corners are right angles.

Row: Things placed side by side. In a table the entries that are in any line across the page.

Sales tax: A percentage added on to the cost of things that are bought. The extra money is then used by the government.

Score: The word for the total in sports and games.

Splitting up: Separating numbers into their part. For example, 67 becomes 60 (just the tens) and 7 (just the units). This makes them easier to work with.

Square number: The number of a collection of objects that can be arranged in a square. It is the product of two equal numbers (for example, 16 is the square number produced from 4 × 4).

Turn-Around Rule: When we add or multiply the same two numbers, the answer is the same no matter which of the numbers comes first (but this does not hold for subtracting or dividing).

Unit: 1 of something. A small, square shape representing 1.

Set index